J
968.97 O'Toole, Thomas   C 2
OT

Malawi in pictures

DISCARDED

DATE DUE

Visual Geography Series®

MALAWI

...in Pictures

Prepared by
Thomas O'Toole

Lerner Publications Company
Minneapolis

VISUAL GEOGRAPHY SERIES®

Publisher
Harry Jonas Lerner
Associate Publisher
Nancy M. Campbell
Senior Editor
Mary M. Rodgers
Editor
Gretchen Bratvold
Assistant Editors
Philip E. Baruth
Dan Filbin
Kathleen S. Heidel
Illustrations Editor
Karen A. Sirvaitis
Consultants/Contributors
Thomas O'Toole
Sandra K. Davis
Designer
Jim Simondet
Cartographer
Carol F. Barrett
Indexer
Sylvia Timian
Production Manager
Gary J. Hansen

Courtesy of Save the Children

A Malawian woman returns from market.

This is an all-new edition of the Visual Geography
Series. Previous editions have been published by Ster-
ling Publishing Company, New York City, and some
of the original textual information has been retained.
New photographs, maps, charts, captions, and updated
information have been added. The text has been entirely reset in 10/12 Century Textbook.

LIBRARY OF CONGRESS CATALOGING-IN-PUBLICATION DATA

O'Toole, Thomas, 1941-

Malawi in pictures / prepared by Thomas O'Toole.
 p. cm.—(Visual geography series)
Rev. ed. of: Malawi in pictures / by Bernadine Bailey.
Includes index.
Summary: Describes the topography, history, society,
economy, and government of the small scenic country
in southeastern Africa.
 ISBN 0-8225-1842-2 (lib. bdg.)
 1. Malawi. [1. Malawi.] I. Bailey, Bernadine, 1901-.
Malawi in pictures. II. Title. III. Series: Visual
geography series (Minneapolis, Minn.)
DT858.086 1988
968.97—dc 19   87–26627
                                          CIP
                                          AC-

International Standard Book Number: 0-8225-1842-2
Library of Congress Card Catalog Number: 87–26627

Courtesy of Malawi High Commission

**Zebras, among other large animals, graze on the high Nyika
Plateau.**

Acknowledgments

Title page photo by Howard W. Mielke.

Elevation contours adapted from *The Times Atlas of
the World,* seventh comprehensive edition (New York:
Times Books, 1985).

2 3 4 5 6 7 8 9 10 97 96 95 94 93 92 91 90 89

Photo by Paul and Bridget Martin

The majority of Malawians live in underdeveloped areas where manufactured goods are scarce. As a result, rural children often fashion their own toys out of metal or wood.

Contents

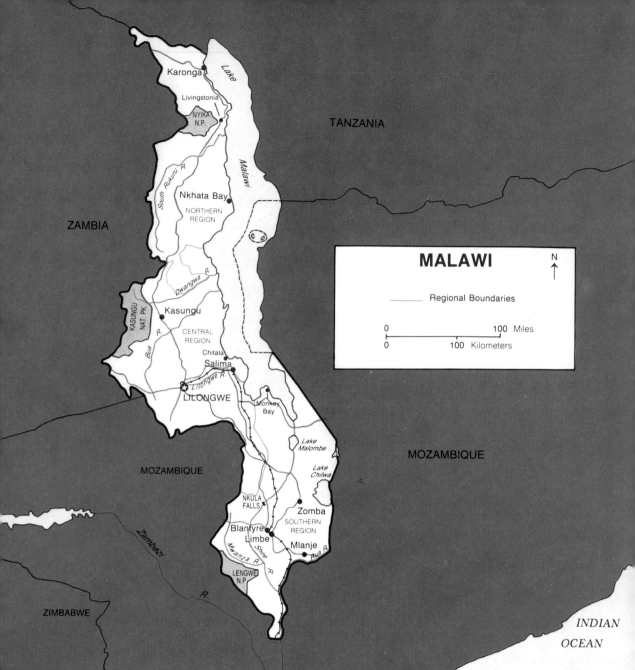

MALAWI

N ↑

Regional Boundaries

| 0 | | 100 Miles |
| 0 | | 100 Kilometers |

TANZANIA

ZAMBIA

MOZAMBIQUE

MOZAMBIQUE

ZIMBABWE

INDIAN OCEAN

Karonga
Livingstonia
NYIKA N.P.
South Rukuru R.
Malawi
Lake
Nkhata Bay
NORTHERN REGION
Dwangwa R.
KASUNGU NAT. PK.
Kasungu
CENTRAL REGION
Bua R.
Chitala
Salima
Lilongwe R.
LILONGWE
Monkey Bay
Lake Malombe
Lake Chilwa
NKULA FALLS
Zomba
SOUTHERN REGION
Blantyre
Limbe
Mlanje
Bua R.
Shire R.
Mwanza R.
LENGWE N.P.
Zambezi
R.

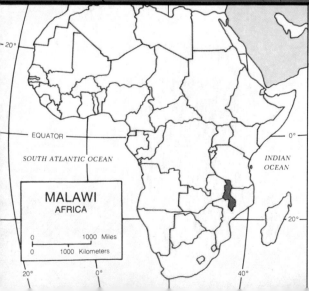

EQUATOR

SOUTH ATLANTIC OCEAN

INDIAN OCEAN

20°

0°

20°

MALAWI
AFRICA

| 0 | | 1000 Miles |
| 0 | | 1000 Kilometers |

20°   0°   40°

METRIC CONVERSION CHART
To Find Approximate Equivalents

WHEN YOU KNOW:	MULTIPLY BY:	TO FIND:
AREA		
acres	0.41	hectares
square miles	2.59	square kilometers
CAPACITY		
gallons	3.79	liters
LENGTH		
feet	30.48	centimeters
yards	0.91	meters
miles	1.61	kilometers
MASS (weight)		
pounds	0.45	kilograms
tons	0.91	metric tons
VOLUME		
cubic yards	0.77	cubic meters
TEMPERATURE		
degrees Fahrenheit	0.56 (*after* subtracting 32)	degrees Celsius

Children and adults alike turn out to greet the boat that brings goods to their village once a week.

Introduction

Malawi—a small, landlocked country in East Africa—was a British colony called Nyasaland from 1891 until it achieved independence in 1964. When it declared self-rule, the nation changed its name to Malawi—the European form of the name Maravi, which refers to an African people who migrated into the region in the thirteenth century. The two largest ethnic groups in the country—the Chewa and the Nyanja—are descendents of the original Maravi people.

Although Malawi has some of the most fertile soil in East Africa, the majority of the nation's people—90 percent of whom live in rural areas—are poor. The lifestyle of the ordinary Malawian has improved little since colonial times. Other former colonies have turned to socialism to solve their pressing social problems. But Hastings Kamuzu Banda—the country's leader since independence—has adopted a Western economic style. His policies emphasize ways of attracting foreign investors and of encouraging Malawian farmers to sell their crops to government-approved organizations. Because the government focuses on the economy, many major problems have been neglected—an issue that Banda has succeeded in keeping out of the press through censorship.

Banda's supporters view the president's policies as successful, pointing to both Malawi's quick repayment of foreign debts and its agricultural self-sufficiency. Banda also continues to pursue economic ties with the white-minority government in South Africa. In return for the president's support, South Africa has funded a number of major development projects in Malawi. The African nations that surround Malawi resent these ties with South Africa's leaders, who support a policy of racial separateness called apartheid. Banda nevertheless insists that his foreign policy is essential to Malawi's survival.

Named life president in 1971, Banda—now in his eighties—continues to hold great popular support, despite social problems and political tensions. Opposition groups have developed outside the country, but none of them has challenged Banda's rule within Malawi. In addition, the president has not named a successor, and this indecision—along with a worsening economy—has increased national concern. Malawi's future may depend on the character of the leader who comes to power after many years of one-person rule.

Malawians—especially the young—enjoy the game of soccer.

Hastings Kamuzu Banda has been Malawi's leader since independence. Banda has been exceptionally popular with rural Malawians, who accord him respect as both a civic leader and a physician.

Funds from the Republic of South Africa have allowed Malawi to build factories to expand its industrial base.

Both the United Nations and the Food and Agriculture Organization provided financial backing for this sugar estate in southern Malawi. Located in the hot and humid lowlands, the land now under cultivation has traditionally been considered unprofitable. The project is one of many designed to upgrade Malawi's agricultural technology.

Small villages, made up of traditional thatch-roofed dwellings, are home to roughly 90 percent of Malawi's people. Houses often surround a shared grain storage bin *(right foreground)*, which may be elevated through the use of long, gnarled poles that act as stilts.

The road to Livingstonia winds through the scenic valleys of the Northern Region. Named for David Livingstone, the Scottish explorer, Livingstonia began as a small mission on the southern tip of Lake Malawi. Scottish missionaries moved the operation to the upper lake area in response to acts of hostility by Yao slave traders.

1) The Land

Wedged between Zambia on the west, Tanzania on the north and east, and Mozambique on the east, south, and west, Malawi is a landlocked nation in southeastern Africa. Long and narrow, the country covers 45,747 square miles, roughly the size of the state of Pennsylvania. From north to south, Malawi stretches for 560 miles; from west to east, its widest span measures 100 miles. Most of the country is quite narrow—at some points barely 30 miles across. The nation is divided into three administrative units—the Northern, Central, and Southern regions.

Topography

A huge rift, or split, which is part of a much larger formation called the Great Rift Valley, dominates Malawi's land surface. This depression, caused by the sinking of the earth's crust millions of years ago, extends from Syria in southwestern Asia to Mozambique in southeastern Africa. The eastern branch of the Great Rift forms a deep trough, which runs the length of Malawi before blending into the plains of Mozambique farther south.

The upper portion of this trough is filled by Lake Malawi, whose northeastern shore forms much of Malawi's border with Tanzania. Part of Malawi's eastern boundary with Mozambique lies within the lake's waters. A series of cliffs and terraces, ranging from low lakeside formations to elevated plateaus, surround the lake on the Malawian shore.

THE SHIRE VALLEY

Lake Malawi's southern shore has crept northward over thousands of years, uncovering an additional 80 miles of the Eastern Rift Valley floor. This area, now called the Upper Shire Valley, is a series of low plains that receive water and silt deposits from the Shire River. Foothills and cliffs still mark the original shoreline of the lake.

The Lower Shire Valley occupies the southernmost portion of the channel cut by the Eastern Rift. Two smaller valleys join the Lower Shire: the Mwanza from the west and the Rua—which drains much of the Shire Plateau—from the east. Despite flooding on the plains and the formation of large swamps, cultivation has increased in this area because of the richness of the soil.

PLATEAUS

Plateaus make up roughly three-fourths of Malawi's land surface. Their fertile, shallow valleys and rolling hills support most of the nation's population. The three major plateaus (sometimes called plains or highlands) are the Nyika Plateau in the Northern Region, the Lilongwe Plain in the Central Region, and the Shire Plateau in the Southern Region.

The Nyika Plateau is the highest plain in the country, standing between 7,000 and 8,000 feet above sea level. Although it covers 9,000 square miles, the Nyika region is sparsely populated and is the least

Photo by Howard W. Mielke

Vegetation is thin and coarse on the slopes of Mount Mlanje. Although Mlanje's higher plateaus are sometimes used for grazing, the soil and climate are not suitable for farming.

9

productive of the three major plateaus. Its elevation brings cool temperatures and prevents the area from receiving much of the river-carried silt and minerals that enrich the southern plains.

The Lilongwe Plain of the Central Region is composed of low hills, valleys, and dambos—areas of moist soil resting on layers of rock. A line of tall granite peaks, which run down from the Northern Region, interrupt the plain's flatness. For the most part, however, elevations range between 2,500 and 4,000 feet above sea level.

The most widely cultivated and settled area in Malawi is the Shire Plateau. With an area of 2,800 square miles, the plain ranges from 2,500 to almost 4,000 feet above sea level. Both the original capital city of Zomba and the largest city, Blantyre, are located in the western portion of this area. The nearby Shire River has traditionally provided both water for farming and a natural route for shipping.

MOUNTAINS
Mountains exist primarily in northern and southern Malawi. Several peaks on the Nyika Plateau reach heights of 8,500 feet. The most impressive range is the Mlanje, which is located in the southernmost portion of the country. Some of the mountains in this range exceed 9,000 feet, and the highest summit—Mount Mlanje—reaches 9,843 feet.

Rivers and Bodies of Water
As a result of its unusual shape, Malawi possesses an efficient watershed system—a series of slopes that guide a country's

Photo by Paul and Bridget Martin

Rising to nearly 10,000 feet above sea level, the highest peaks of the Mlanje Mountains remain barren throughout the year. Although much of Malawi is located at elevations high enough to bring cooler temperatures, only the Mlanje range receives seasonal snowfall.

Malawi's Shire River—which provides drainage for the entire country— changes character depending on its location. Between the Upper and Lower Shire valleys, the waterway runs very quickly, and rapids make travel by boat impossible.

In the Upper Shire Valley, the Shire River is calm and navigable.

rivers to a lake or ocean. From the Northern Region to the Central Region, the South Rukuru, Dwangwa, Bua, and Lilongwe rivers run eastward into Lake Malawi. Lake Malawi and rivers in the Southern Region flow into the Shire River. The Shire deposits silt on the many floodplains of the Southern Region before it runs into the Zambezi River in Mozambique.

Also known as Lake Nyasa, Lake Malawi occupies 11,000 square miles, roughly one-fourth of Malawi's total area. About 355 miles long and 59 miles across at its widest point, Lake Malawi is the third largest body of water in Africa after Lakes Victoria and Tanganyika. The average depth of Lake Malawi is 2,250 feet. Cliffs rise to 2,000 feet near the shoreline in some areas, and over 200 species of fish flourish in the lake's waters.

The Shire River begins at Lake Malawi and runs south through Lake Malombe—a shallow, 18-mile-long body of water. At a steep section of rocky hills and cliffs, midway between the Upper and Lower Shire valleys, the river's elevation drops 1,200 feet in just 60 miles. Rapids and rough water make travel hazardous. The Shire

11

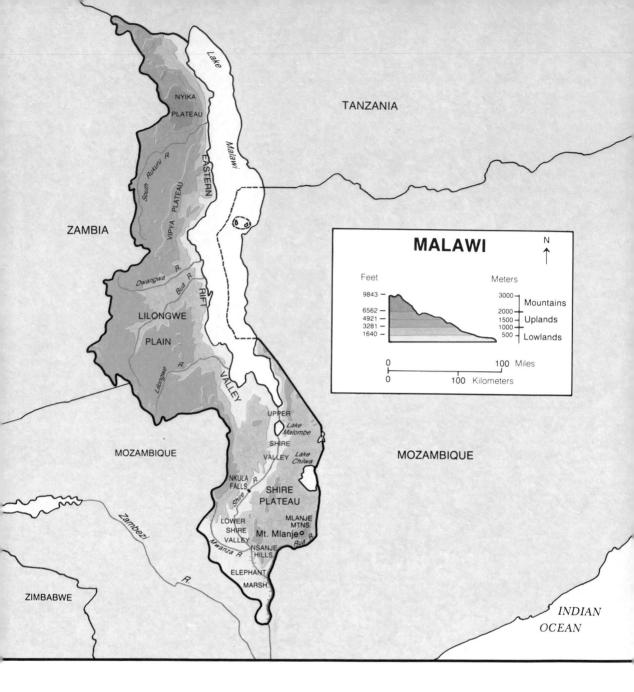

passes over the Murchison Rapids and Nkula Falls before reaching the Lower Shire Valley. Water and valuable silts from the north and west collect in sluggish swamplands, such as Elephant Marsh—a huge wetland that is 40 miles long and 9 miles wide.

After passing through the lower part of the valley, the Shire River flows into Mozambique's Zambezi River, which empties into the Indian Ocean. Apart from some smaller, southeastern streams, which feed into Lake Chilwa and its surrounding marshes, the Shire and its tributaries drain the entire country.

Climate

Although Malawi lies in the tropics near the equator, the country's high altitude keeps it from being uncomfortably hot and humid. In most places, the climate is pleasantly cool much of the year.

Temperatures at high elevations—5,000 to 8,000 feet—range from daytime maximums of 92° F to nighttime lows of 32° F in the Mlanje Mountains and other uplands. Midlevel elevations (approximately 3,500 feet above sea level) record temperatures from 80° F to 90° F in November and from 40° F to 50° F in July. The low areas of the Shire Valley and some locations near Lake Malawi are the hottest and most humid in the country. Only about 200 feet above sea level, these areas have an average temperature of 89° F, with a maximum above 100° F. Humidity at this elevation hovers at roughly 80 percent throughout the year.

From May to October, little rain falls, and, in the one long rainy season from November to April, rainfall varies. The Shire River Valley and the shores of Lake Malawi receive 25 to 35 inches a year. Between 100 and 130 inches a year fall in the highlands.

In early 1989, rainfall and other factors caused massive flooding in populated sections of Malawi. Thousands of Malawian families lost their farms and houses in the disaster. Many temporary residents— many of whom were refugees from Mozambique's civil war—also became homeless. Experts believe that the flooding will seriously affect Malawi's farming productivity.

Flora and Fauna

Savanna woodlands—a mixture of scrub, thorn, coarse grasses, and widely scattered trees—cover most of Malawi. Dense forests replace the savanna only in wet areas, such as Nkhata Bay, the northern Nsanje Hills, and the Mlanje Mountains to the south. These forests are a mixture of evergreen and deciduous (leaf-shedding) trees. Baobab trees, marked by twisted branches and gray, barkless trunks, dot the landscape. At lower altitudes, mahogany and palms are common.

Also in the lowlands—or in naturally wet areas such as dambos—marsh grasses, sedge, and reeds abound. These plants provide grazing for cattle and wildlife during the dry months, when the savanna is bare of plants. Some families have cleared dambos and marshes and have converted them to small farm plots. Traditional slash-and-burn farming techniques—which involve clearing a new field every few years by cutting down the vegetation and setting small

Photo by Paul and Bridget Martin

Manchewe is one of Malawi's steepest waterfalls.

13

Malawi's animal life includes several species of antelope, such as these impalas, which are noted for extraordinary quickness and agility.

The baobab tree—known for its massive trunk and gray-black, spindly branches—makes use of a large root system, which anchors and nourishes the tree even in thin soil.

brush fires—have destroyed much of Malawi's plant life.

Compared to other countries of eastern and southern Africa, Malawi has little animal life. The number of people has grown quickly over the past two decades, causing the amount of grazing land to decrease. The remaining animal population continues to shrink as Malawians con-vert more savanna to farmland. Neverthe-less, many species of antelope, along with lions, zebras, cheetahs, buffalo, and ele-phants, populate unsettled regions. Vast game preserves have been set up to help increase wildlife populations.

On the plateaus, some mammals—in-cluding leopards, bushbuck, wild pigs, and baboons—continue to roam freely. A

Courtesy of Malawi High Commission

Because of shrinking animal habitats in Malawi, African elephants *(above)* are now found primarily in remote Kasungu district. Malawi's water-ways attract both exotic and familiar bird-life *(right).*

Independent Picture Service

15

The hyena *(above)* is one of the fiercest animals that still roams the nation in plentiful numbers. Lions have become quite scarce in recent decades, while hippopotamuses survive only in the small lagoons surrounding Lake Malawi.

Related to both the stork and the heron, the hammerkop is a brown wading bird native to East Africa.

varied birdlife also exists, ranging from familiar species like the sparrow and the owl to more exotic tropical varieties. Over 200 species of fish swim in Malawi's waters, including *mpasa,* or lake salmon.

Common reptiles include the tortoise and the crocodile, as well as poisonous snakes such as the hooded cobra. Mosquitoes and other disease-carrying insects present a serious health hazard. Tsetse flies, carriers of the virus that causes sleeping sickness, threaten livestock in 12 percent of the nation.

Cities

Only 12 percent of Malawi's people live in urban areas, where there is paid employment. The southern third of the country contains more than half of the total population, because of the richness of the soil.

Malawi's largest city, Blantyre, covers an area of 83 square miles in the Southern

Malawians have long used the aloe plant, an offshoot of the lily family, as a medicine.

Lilongwe, Malawi's capital city, is the newest urban center in the country. Many of the government structures were built prior to 1975 with extensive financial support from the Republic of South Africa.

Blantyre is Malawi's largest metropolis and the financial and commercial capital of the nation.

Many of Blantyre's streets *(right)* have not changed since the early twentieth century. During this period, British officials imposed heavy taxes, enabling them to build elegant colonial residences *(below).*

The road connecting Blantyre and Zomba runs past many small, traditional villages, emphasizing the very limited urban influence in the country.

Region and includes the two communities of Blantyre and Limbe, which are five miles apart. Together they have a population of over 250,000. Blantyre is the country's main commercial, industrial, and communications hub. Housing in Blantyre includes upper- and middle-class accommodations, like those found in prosperous sections of urban centers throughout the world. There is also the more traditional African pattern of round houses with thatched roofs. Slum dwellings of cardboard and tin exist as well.

Lilongwe, the capital of Malawi, took over 10 years to build and cost over $15 million. Loans from the Republic of South Africa helped to fund construction of the city, which in 1975 replaced Zomba as the nation's capital. With a population of over 100,000, Lilongwe is Malawi's second largest city. Lilongwe lies between 3,400 and 3,600 feet above sea level, and, because of

the altitude, the climate is fairly temperate. The temperature varies from an average of 74° F in the winter to 86° F in the summer. The failure of city planners to anticipate the problems of the capital's large population has resulted in crowded streets and poor-quality housing.

Zomba is located about 60 miles north of Blantyre, on the Shire Plateau. Zomba is the country's third largest city (population 50,000) and a center for light industry and agricultural trade. Many old structures still stand as reminders of the period when Malawi was a British colony. The State House, whose foundation was laid in 1901, and the Old Residency stand beside modern medical and educational buildings. Zomba was developed as a university town after Lilongwe became the capital. The main campus of the University of Malawi and the National Archives of Malawi are both located in Zomba.

Independence Arch is one of many monuments honoring those who served in the fight for national self-rule.

2) History and Government

Archaeologists believe that Malawi has been inhabited by humankind for at least 60,000 years. Eventually two main groups —the ancestors of the Kafula people and a group of Bantu-speakers—occupied and farmed the Malawi region before the Maravi people migrated there in the late thirteenth century.

The Maravi

Led southward and eastward from the Zaire River Basin by their leader, Mazizi, the Maravi were the first large group to enter the area around Lake Malawi. The group split into several smaller units after the death of Mazizi. By the sixteenth century the main body of the Maravi dominated the southern and western regions, including the Shire River Valley.

Two groups—the Katanga and the Kafula—already occupied the area to the southwest of the lake. Peaceful Bantu-speakers, the Katanga were easily absorbed by the Maravi. The nomadic (migratory) Kafula, who had settled around the lake, fought the Maravi with iron-tipped darts that they coated with poison. Eventually, the Maravi drove the Kafula into what are now the nations of Zambia and Mozambique.

The ruling Maravi leader granted the land west of Lake Malawi to two smaller Maravi communities, which together became known as the Chewa. By the end of the sixteenth century, the Chewa and other Maravi peoples had developed long-distance trade contacts with Kilwa, a coastal trading center located in present-day Tanzania.

The Maravi, who had united under a single leader, reached the height of their power in the seventeenth century. They vied for goods against growing numbers of competitors, such as the Portuguese, who had begun to take away the Maravi's traditional trade in ivory and other items.

The Swahili—a people of mixed African and Arab descent—posed additional competition. They ran slaves and goods from their villages on the east coast of Africa to the island of Zanzibar, which was a center of the Arabian slave trade.

Loss of trade, combined with the long distances between the various groups and their main ruler, weakened the centralized authority of the Maravi Empire. By 1800 powerful local leaders were bargaining with the Portuguese for their own weapons and soon were fully independent of their ties to the empire.

The Ngoni

In the early 1800s African refugees began to migrate northward to escape the forces of Shaka, the Zulu leader who was taking

Ngoni men, in historical clothing, dance in remembrance of Ngoni migrations from South Africa that occurred during the nineteenth century.

Independent Picture Service

over lands and peoples in South Africa. In 1835 one of these refugee groups, the Jere Ngoni, crossed the Zambezi River and moved north into Malawi. Under Zwangendaba, their leader, the Jere Ngoni conquered and absorbed the peoples they met on their journey.

The Maseko Ngoni, a related group that also moved north to escape the Zulu, circled Lake Malawi before settling west of the lake. The stronger Maseko Ngoni absorbed the Chewa, and their combined armies drove out the warlike Yao, who were the area's most active slave traders. Although the Ngoni ruled, they adopted the language of the more numerous Chewa.

The Slave Trade

Until the beginning of the nineteenth century, the slave trade in Malawi existed mostly among local groups. Warriors captured in battle were kept or sold to other villages. On rare occasions, a Portuguese ship would raid the Lower Shire Valley and would carry Africans away as slaves.

Nineteenth-century British policy was committed to ending the slave trade. In 1817 Radama I, the king of the Merina people on the island of Madagascar, signed an agreement put forward by the British government to slow Madagascar's slave trade. This event significantly cut the flow of slaves from the east coast to Egypt, Arabia, and the nations around the Persian Gulf. As a result, coastal slave traders, principally the Yao, moved toward the African interior, where they captured many Maravi. The captives were sent in long slave caravans to ships on the east coast.

The westward movement of the slave traders was checked when the Maseko

Swahili and Arab slave traders moved slaves captured from the African interior—including Malawi—to Swahili villages on the east coast. From these ports, African slaves were often shipped to the island of Zanzibar, a major slave-trading center.

22

Ngoni moved into the Lilongwe Plain and lake area around 1860. Unlike the splintered Maravi, this Ngoni group had an excellent military organization. The Yao peoples, who now lacked the slaves they needed to exchange for weapons, began to supply slaves from their own population.

The Missionaries

A Scottish missionary and explorer, David Livingstone, reached the Lake Malawi region in the mid-nineteenth century. Livingstone was searching for a trade route that would be profitable enough to replace the slave trade. He also believed that the new traders in the region would fund Christian missions throughout the African interior. Between 1858 and 1863, Livingstone ventured into the area four times. He mapped the Shire River Valley and Lake Malawi (which he called Lake Nyasa) for the first time in 1859. Largely as a result of the explorer's influence, committees from four universities established the Universities Mission to Central Africa (UMCA).

At this stage, the British government was more interested in temporary, profitable trade than in acquiring colonies, which were considered expensive and troublesome to maintain. Livingstone's search for a faster trade route fit the economic plans of the British government, and it invested in his expeditions. Later, Great Britain used Livingstone's discoveries and influence to claim African territory.

The main goal of Lord Palmerston, the British prime minister at that time, was to establish communication that would lead to safer trade routes. He sent Livingstone to Quelimane near Lake Malawi in 1858 as a British representative. Livingstone's orders were to contact the African leaders of the interior. By setting up the first mission in the Shire Plateau in 1861, Livingstone made Malawi a center for Christian missionary activity in Central Africa.

A detail from J. M. W. Turner's painting *The Slave Ship* shows slaves being drowned at sea.

Explorer David Livingstone was one of Great Britain's chief antislavery figures. Livingstone's lectures spurred both missionary and governmental efforts on behalf of African slaves.

Effects of the Missions

The missions produced rapid educational results and thrived economically even after Livingstone's death in 1873. The

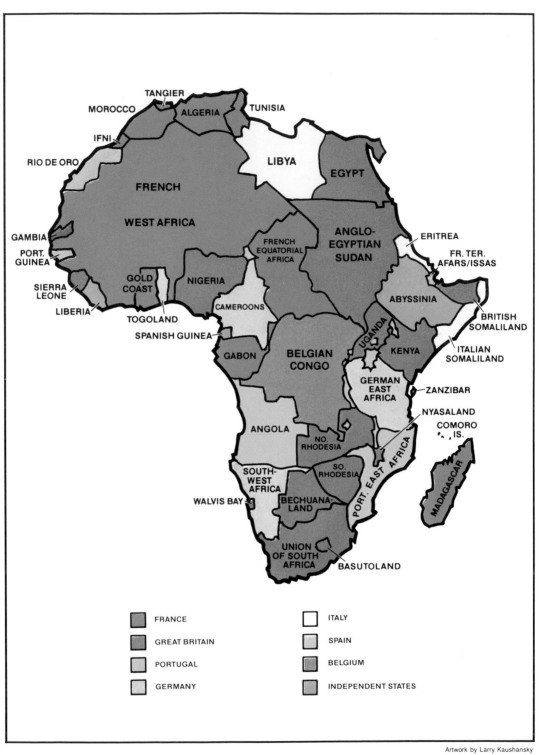

Artwork by Larry Kaushansky

By the late nineteenth century, European powers had carved the continent of Africa into their own areas of influence. Present-day Malawi was called Nyasaland and was administered by the British as a protectorate until 1964. (Map information taken from *The Anchor Atlas of World History,* 1978.)

Zambezi Industrial Mission had over 35,000 acres of coffee under cultivation in 1893. By 1885 the Livingstonia missions had 35 schools in operation. At these institutions Africans learned trades such as carpentry and agriculture along with Christianity and the English language.

The desire to spread Christianity and the urge to exploit the wealth of Africa were sometimes hard to distinguish. Missionaries wanted to halt the slave trade for humanitarian reasons. European businesspeople wanted to stop the trade because it was taking away both customers for their imported goods and labor for their plantations.

Slowly, local ethnic groups lost their trade customers to Europeans. The traditional role of African groups of the interior—to carry goods to and from the coast—had often rested on their ability to pass safely through hostile territory. But the Europeans built new rail lines and ran armed steamships on Lake Malawi, which enabled them to move large amounts of goods safely and more quickly.

Unfortunately, Livingstone's exploration of the Shire River served to increase the slave trade by showing Swahili and Portuguese traders a way to move ocean-going ships into the Upper Shire Valley. Although the missionaries were well meaning, they knew little of the land and culture of the African peoples among whom they lived.

The Scramble for Africa

The presence of the British in the Malawi area aroused the interest of other Western powers. They became concerned that they might get only a small portion of the potentially valuable African lands. Although the British, French, and Portuguese had been exploring Africa and claiming various parts of it, most of the continent was still unmapped. In the 1880s, however, Belgium and Germany came on the scene, and soon a rush—often called the scramble for Africa—began. Countries hurried to stake claims and to establish control over huge areas that had not yet been explored.

During the following decade of European expansion, local ethnic groups found themselves suddenly both courted and threatened by many European countries. In general, European governments could not support claims to land unless they could prove their interest there. The easiest proof of such interest was a treaty between a European power and a local leader. Again missionaries became useful to government officials. The British missionaries were convinced that British rule would benefit the Africans, and they used their regional influence to establish treaties.

Local leaders were often offered yearly payments, protection by the foreign government, and weapons in exchange for their signatures. In certain situations, leaders who signed a treaty with one country would be attacked by another nation. As a result, the attacked leader would sign a new agreement.

Though the British government pledged to obtain land only by mutual consent, it fought the Chewa, the Maseko Ngoni, and the Yao. The British signed treaties with these peoples after defeating them in battle. In spite of European promises to protect rather than to take over territory, African influence was lost.

Photo by Paul and Bridget Martin

Livingstonia missions still operate throughout Malawi.

Geography, as well as European treaties, determined the shape of the colony that is now independent Malawi. Lake Malawi formed the region's eastern border, and British treaties or land grants determined all other frontiers. In dividing up the African continent, the Europeans established boundaries that separated traditional communities. Many ethnic groups were split among British, Portuguese, and German rulers. In Malawi this situation prevented the Africans from having a powerful voice in their country's national affairs.

Nyasaland Districts Protectorate

In 1889 Britain sent its representative Sir Harry Johnston to Mozambique to protest Portuguese attempts to control the flow of traffic on the Zambezi River. Johnston had already spent considerable time in Africa, and he knew several African languages. He was able to make treaties with the leaders of the various regions of Malawi.

Early in 1889 Johnston had met a businessman named Cecil Rhodes, who felt that Great Britain should occupy a huge strip—from Egypt to South Africa—on the African continent. Rhodes wanted his own company, the British South Africa Company, to govern this territory. Rhodes

promised to pay Johnston's expenses if he would collect the necessary signatures of the leaders in the Malawi region. Although the scheme fell through, the treaty signatures that Johnston obtained helped to establish British regional dominance.

In May 1891 Britain proclaimed a protectorate—called the Nyasaland Districts Protectorate—over the large area north of the Zambezi River. The colony included areas that are now the nations of Malawi, Zimbabwe, and Zambia. Harry Johnston was appointed the first consul-general of the protectorate and held wide governmental powers.

One of Johnston's first tasks was to end the slave trade and to impose British rule at the southern end of Lake Malawi, where Yao slave traders still raided the countryside. He built Fort Johnston as a southern base and freed 270 slaves who were about to be sent to the coast. The Yao leaders, however, intensified their raiding and military attacks.

Although the battles against the Yao were chiefly over the issue of slavery, other factors were involved. For example, the Yao had refused to negotiate with the British, who were determined to impose their authority. Extra colonial forces were sent from Cape Town in South Africa, and with them Johnston attacked the fighters of the Yao leader, Makanjira. Although

British troops, highly organized and heavily armed, eventually defeated all resistance from Nyasaland's ethnic groups.

Makanjira's village was destroyed twice, he escaped to Portuguese territory. The British finally broke the power of the Yao slave traders in December 1895 and began to occupy the southern part of the colony of Nyasaland.

After virtually eliminating the slave trade in Nyasaland, Harry Johnston set up a British-style government throughout the colony. He divided the country into districts and put each one under the control of an official, or magistrate. In addition, he brought in tax collectors, an accountant, a medical officer, and a group of surveyors who marked boundaries and laid out roads. Johnston chose Zomba as the capital and had a large colonial home built there.

Conflicts Within the Protectorate

Suffering from black fever, Johnston left the protectorate in 1897 and was replaced by Alfred Sharpe. Although Sharpe had fewer problems with the Yao and Arab slave traders, he inherited an odd financial situation from Johnston's administration. When the protectorate over the Nyasaland districts had been proclaimed in 1891, the British government decided against paying the new administration's expenses. In exchange for exclusive mining rights in the colony, Cecil Rhodes had funded the Nyasaland government through his British South Africa Company.

Because Rhodes's company was paying the colony's administrative expenses, Rhodes felt entitled to a large voice in the operation of the protectorate. Friction developed between the new government and the charter company. In 1902 a British commission formally widened the powers of the protectorate's commissioner. Sharpe was given charge of leasing or granting lands, of controlling all mineral rights, and of deporting subjects according to his own judgment.

In 1907 the territory was renamed the Nyasaland Protectorate, and executive

Independent Picture Service

Cecil Rhodes extended British civil and commercial rule throughout much of southern and eastern Africa, which he straddles in this period cartoon.

and legislative councils were established. Neither of these councils had African members, but one missionary was permitted to sit on the Legislative Council to speak for the Africans.

Although the missionaries educated a number of Africans, the government of the protectorate arranged no system of education for local peoples. White planters on the ruling councils called for house taxes, which Africans could afford to pay only by working on European-owned plantations. In 1901, for example, an African farmer could avoid paying the house tax only by substituting four months of labor.

Early Resistance to British Rule

The small number of educated Africans in Nyasaland were trained mostly as guides and interpreters. There were exceptions, however. John Chilembwe, a Yao, was educated in both Nyasaland and the United

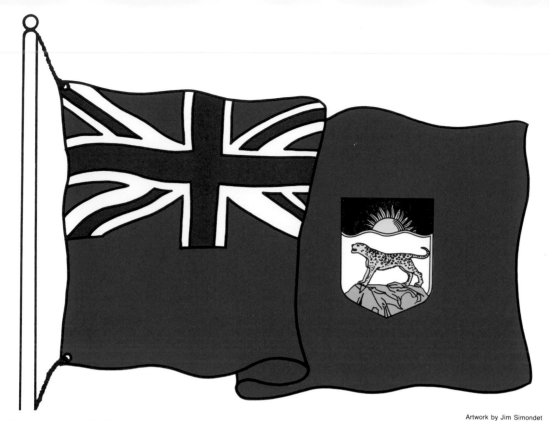

Nyasaland's colonial flag came into use in 1911 and continued as the protectorate's emblem until 1953.

States. One of Chilembwe's early influences in Nyasaland was Joseph Booth, the founder of the Zambezi Industrial Mission. Booth was eventually pressured to leave Nyasaland because he spoke out in support of African nationalism. He taught his students, Chilembwe among them, that Africa should belong to Africans.

After returning to Nyasaland in 1900, Chilembwe established a number of African schools and became head of an independent African church in the Southern Region. Taking advantage of all legal channels, he began to push for better conditions for African workers.

Because improvements were slow in coming, Chilembwe felt that a show of force—even a weak show of force—was necessary to draw attention to the problems the Africans faced. He and a small number of followers staged what Europeans called the Native Rising of 1915. During the revolt, Chilembwe was killed by government troops, which quickly sup-

pressed the movement. Chilembwe's effort, however, helped to form a new national identity by breaking down the traditional barriers between ethnic groups. Chilembwe is remembered as the first African in Malawi to die protesting British rule.

African Associations

In addition to Chilembwe's movement, a number of other African political associations also developed in the early twentieth century. The membership of these organizations was primarily mission-educated and included all ethnic groups. The first Native Association was established in 1912 at Karonga. Between 1912 and the 1930s nine other regional groups were formed. These groups worked for government representation and better working conditions for Africans.

In the mid-1930s the government attempted to weaken the associations by insisting that requests for political changes pass through complicated government channels. Despite this restriction, several groups maintained direct contact with government officials.

The outbreak of World War II—along with the drafting of Malawian soldiers—delayed the formation of a nationwide association. But in 1943, when the threat of a prolonged war had passed Nyasaland, James Frederick Sangala proposed the formation of an African council. In October 1944 the Nyasaland African Congress (NAC) became the colony's first nationwide African organization. Seventeen ethnic associations joined the NAC as branch members.

But members soon accused the NAC of dishonest management and of favoring certain ethnic groups. Consequently, the association lost the popular support that it had been building. Thus weakened, the NAC was unable to protest effectively against the British government's plan to federate (combine) the colonies of Northern Rhodesia, Southern Rhodesia, and Nyasaland—the modern nations of Zambia, Zimbabwe, and Malawi.

The Central African Federation

From the early 1900s onward, European settlers in Southern Rhodesia had been calling for the British government to federate the three colonies. Whites in Nyasaland and Northern Rhodesia were originally opposed to the idea. They felt that Southern Rhodesia, the richest of the three colonies, would eventually gain control over the federation.

The severe economic depression of the early 1930s, however, changed the financial picture in Africa. Federation now seemed to promise stronger colonial economies. In addition, many European settlers had come to regard Africa as their permanent home. Nyasaland settlers felt that joining with Southern Rhodesia—and its large white population—would provide them greater security. Debate over federation also helped to push the British South Africa Company out of Nyasaland's affairs, giving Great Britain complete control over the colony's government.

In Nyasaland, as well as among Africans in Great Britain, a campaign to resist federation began. Most African groups felt

The rising sun from Nyasaland's flag—joined by the lion of Southern Rhodesia's flag and the white waves from the flag of Northern Rhodesia—appeared on the coat of arms of the Central African Federation. The federation combined the three territories into one political unit until 1963.

Artwork by Jim Simondet

29

Malawians began to migrate to other parts of Africa in search of work in the early twentieth century when British taxes proved too steep for small-scale farmers to pay. A large segment of migrant workers labored in the mines of Southern Rhodesia (modern Zimbabwe) and South Africa. Miners, having lived under pro-white rule in these nations, feared the federation of Southern Rhodesia, Northern Rhodesia (now Zambia), and Nyasaland and worked to prevent unification. In addition, poor working conditions in Africa's mines became a separate issue for African nationalists.

that their ethnic identity would be lost by the change, and they feared the strongly pro-white policies of Southern Rhodesia. Despite protest, the British formed the Central African Federation on August 1, 1953.

Africans soon united in political action against the new federation. This unity might have taken longer to come about had there not been such a clear rallying point. The question of federation made politics a living issue in the village as well as in the city.

The NAC

The federation debate brought the first real demands for Africans to rule themselves. The NAC regained numbers and strength and by April 1957 claimed to have over 60,000 members. Two new leaders of the NAC—Henry B. M. Chipembere and Kanyama Chiume—fostered much of this growth. Both men had studied outside of Nyasaland and had returned to aid the struggle against federation.

The NAC developed the symbols of a mass political party—a slogan of *Kwaca*

In the 1970s, Hastings Banda visited British prime minister Edward Heath at Number 10 Downing Street, the prime minister's official residence in London. After being made life president, Banda continued to pursue a pro-British foreign policy.

(the dawn), a national flag, and a weekly newsletter—and glorified the activities of John Chilembwe. The party, however, still lacked an experienced leader with popular appeal. The congress turned to Hastings Kamuzu Banda.

Hastings Kamuzu Banda

Throughout the troubled years of Malawi's bid for nationhood, Hastings Banda watched the political developments from abroad. Born in the Kasungu area of Malawi in 1906, Banda was mission-educated. After holding several jobs in South Africa and Rhodesia, he came to the attention of a group of U.S. missionaries. They sent him to the United States, where he attended high school and college and where he became a physician in 1937.

Banda stayed in Great Britain during World War II and soon had a good medical practice in London. His home became the meeting place of Africans who lived in Great Britain, and he became involved in African politics. Not until 1958, however, did Banda return to his homeland. At that time, the young leadership of the NAC invited him to assume control of their orga-

nization. The NAC leaders hoped to use Banda's professional image and experience to unite the people.

Banda was so successful in gaining local support that just one year after he had been invited to head the NAC, the colonial authorities declared a state of emergency. They put Banda in jail and tried to suppress the African nationalist movement, which was gaining momentum throughout the continent.

Although the NAC used nonviolent methods when it began, disturbances, rioting, and violence became frequent in the 1950s. The party was banned, and Banda's supporters formed the Malawi Congress party (MCP) to take its place. Faced with increased governmental restrictions, African opposition grew. In 1961, to quiet the situation, the British released Banda and invited him to London for a constitutional conference. In the elections that followed the conference, Banda's MCP won by an overwhelming majority.

Independence

After the 1961 elections, Great Britain insisted that full independence would be

Republic Day celebrations *(above)* mark the anniversary of Malawi's independence on July 6, 1964. The Young Pioneers—a national youth group founded by Banda—regularly perform at state celebrations, demonstrating complex gymnastic routines. President Banda *(right),* waving a fly whisk—an African symbol of leadership—was once known for his cross-country tours to gain the political support of the Malawian people. In recent years, however, Banda's advanced age has prevented further tours.

based on a demonstration of responsible self-government. During 1961 and 1962, Malawians showed their ability to manage their own affairs. The MCP then took full control of the country's administration. A revised constitution was agreed upon, and Nyasaland became the independent state of Malawi on July 6, 1964.

Representing a conservative form of African nationalism, Banda's government defeated opposition from the progressive, mission-educated elite within two months of independence. In September 1964 Banda forced six cabinet members to resign after they demanded a foreign policy that supported other colonies who were fighting for independence. A white-led police force and army harassed those who disagreed with the government's direction.

An unsuccessful internal revolt, led by one of Banda's opponents from the Yao ethnic group, broke out in 1965. Two years later a former minister organized another attack against the government. The unstable situation led Banda to declare a state of national emergency and to accept an appointment as life president.

Relations with Africa

In the 1970s Malawi became an outcast in black Africa by choosing to retain ties with the Republic of South Africa, whose policy of racial separation, called apartheid, has offended many black nations. South Africa rewarded Malawi with aid and loans to build the new capital in Lilongwe and to construct a rail link to the Indian Ocean. These projects have given the Malawian economy a greater appearance of prosperity. President Banda's answer to critics of this policy is that South Africa is too strong for Malawi to attack, and thus diplomatic channels must be kept open to promote black-majority rule in South Africa.

President Banda has also been criticized for his aggressive approach to neighboring Tanzania and Zambia. The primary cause for tension came late in 1964, when several cabinet ministers—whom Banda believed to be in rebellion against him— fled to Zambia and Tanzania. Both countries refused to return the ministers to Malawi, where they had been sentenced to death. President Banda responded by

Apartheid (meaning apartness), which Malawi's president has recently criticized, is a South African policy designed to separate racial groups from one another on both professional and social levels.

making public claims to vast portions of land in Tanzania and Zambia. Although these claims were never acted upon, Zambia and Tanzania became more careful in their relations with the Banda administration.

Banda has encouraged farmers and craftspeople to sell their products only through government-sponsored organizations, such as this lumber cooperative near Mount Mlanje.

Workers on a large-scale tobacco plantation do nearly all of their planting, weeding, and picking by hand. Foreign investors usually continue this system, because the large numbers of available rural workers make hand labor inexpensive.

Critics found further fault with Banda's refusal to cut economic ties with the government of Zimbabwe (then Southern Rhodesia) when it was dominated by a white minority. Banda's reasoning was that economic sanctions would increase the hostility between whites in power and the black majority. He felt instead that Malawi should provide a model of peaceful ethnic cooperation. Relations with Zimbabwe in the late 1980s were strained, as were Malawi's relations with most black-majority regimes in the region.

The Late 1980s

Continuing civil conflict in Mozambique poses a grave threat to Malawi's stability. A rebel group called the Mozambique National Resistance (RENAMO), which receives financial support from South Africa, has been systematically destroying the railroads that carry Mozambique's goods to port. Unfortunately these same rail lines provide Malawi's only inexpensive route to the sea. South Africa's support of RENAMO is hurting Malawi's economy.

Blantyre, shown here in an aerial photograph taken in the mid-1970s, continues to expand through foreign investment.

34

High barbed-wire fences protect the headquarters *(left)* of the Malawi Congress party (MCP). The MCP is the only legal political party in Malawi. Blantyre's European-style town hall *(below),* is used more for social events than for government business.

Consequently, Banda has improved relations with Malawi's neighbors and has initiated mutual economic and diplomatic projects. Banda also has begun openly to criticize the government of South Africa. He has expressed regret over his longstanding relations with the minority regime but holds to the belief that his country's economic survival requires it. Tensions in southeastern Africa remain high and may be heightened by concern over a successor to the president, who turned 83 in 1989.

In early April 1985 President Banda dissolved his cabinet and temporarily took over all the administrative posts himself. Though the cabinet was later reassembled, Banda gave no explanations for this action. In addition, the administrative post of secretary-general of the MCP has remained unfilled since 1983, which suggests that Banda does not intend to let any other political leader acquire a base of power in the country.

Government

The Constitution of 1966 gives supreme executive authority to the president and allows this person to select a cabinet from

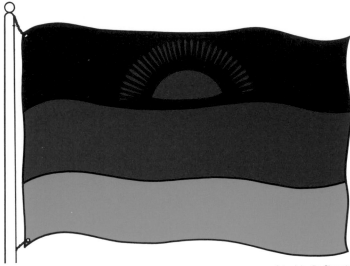

The flag of the MCP—consisting of black, red, and green bars—served as the basis for Malawi's national flag. After independence, a red sunburst was added to symbolize hope both for the new nation and for other African nations fighting for independence.

Artwork by Jim Simondet

within or outside of the legislature. Banda was made life president through a special amendment to the original constitution. In 1987 the president's cabinet consisted of 12 members. Ministers head departments and run the three regions into which the country is divided. The speaker of Parliament is nominated by the president, who also selects a candidate for each of the 60 districts of Malawi. Since the Malawi Congress party is the only legal party in the country, any candidate it nominates gains office without opposition.

A supreme court of appeal is the highest court in Malawi's judicial system. Three to five judges, headed by a chief justice, make up this body. Just below the supreme court is a high court, which can try both civil and criminal cases. Two entirely separate lower courts—magistrate's courts and traditional courts—complete Malawi's judiciary.

Photo by Paul and Bridget Martin

Large, colonial-style residences still serve as reminders of the wealth and political power that European nations acquired in Africa.

Malawian schoolchildren are required to learn English, but many also speak Chichewa.

3) The People

Malawi's 7.7 million people are 99 percent African. In the late 1980s Europeans made up less than one-third of 1 percent of the total population, and Asians numbered less than one-half of 1 percent. English remains the official language of Malawi, although Chichewa became a national language in 1968 and is understood by roughly three-fourths of the population. A range of other Bantu-related languages are also spoken.

Population Characteristics

Almost 90 percent of Malawians still live in rural villages. The population is distrib- uted very unevenly, with more than half of the total living in the Southern Region, which has the nation's three largest cities —Blantyre, Zomba, and Lilongwe. The Northern Region has only 12 percent of the people, and the Central Region has 36 percent.

Malawi has more people per square mile than any other country in Central Africa. The nation averages 168 people per square mile, compared with 26 in Zambia and 48 in Mozambique.

After the slave trade and the disruptions of the nineteenth century came to an end, the population increased at a fast pace. In the mid-1980s, the annual growth rate was

Although Banda's administration has been criticized for favoring his own ethnic group, in general the president has struggled to enforce a sense of unity in Malawi. Children learn English as a common tongue and speak local dialects only in their homes or villages.

3.2 percent, among the highest in Africa. If it continues to grow at this rate, Malawi's population will double in just over 20 years.

Ethnic Groups

The ethnic composition of present-day Malawi has changed greatly in the last century. A variety of ethnic groups—including the Ngoni, Yao, and Tonga—have lived in Malawi only since the late 1800s. The present government discourages ethnic loyalties. Consequently, the nation's people have become less conscious of their regional traditions.

The Chewa and Nyanja—both descended from the Maravi who migrated to present-day Malawi in the thirteenth century—together make up over 50 percent of the population. Both groups speak Chichewa, a language that was originally called Chinyanja, after the Nyanja people. The government changed the name when the first census after independence showed that the Chewa were the largest group speaking Chinyanja. The Nyanja saw this move as the beginning of political domination by the Chewa and have resisted the change.

The Chewa are the more numerous of the two peoples and dominate Lilongwe, Dedza, Nkhota Kota, and other districts of the Central Region. The Nyanja, whose name means "people of the lake," outnumber other groups of the Southern Region, which includes Lake Chilwa and the southern shore of Lake Malawi.

Occupying the eastern part of the Southern Region, the Lomwe represent one-fifth of Malawi's population. Many of the Lomwe in Malawi are migrant workers from Mozambique who come seasonally in search of employment on the tea or cotton estates. A sizable number of these people have settled into a life of rice cultivation within Malawi's borders.

The Yao, Ngoni, Tumbuka, Tonga, Sena, Ngonde, Asian, and European peoples together form roughly 25 percent of the population. Figures for the Tonga and Yao are difficult to verify because, like the Lomwe, they travel outside the country in search of better economic prospects. Many Yao are employed in Zimbabwe's mines or in Zambia's agricultural industries.

Migratory Workers

In the colonial era, Malawian workers moved into surrounding countries to earn money to pay British house taxes. Since then, migratory workers have continued to participate in the cash economies of other countries, which allows them to send money back to their families or to purchase consumer goods.

Malawian migrant workers traditionally have labored in the mines and fields of Zimbabwe, Zambia, and South Africa. In the mid-1970s over 300,000 Malawians left the country to find employment. About 60 percent of all Malawian men have worked outside the country at least once.

Although gone for long periods of time, the majority of workers continue to participate in family decisions by mail. When they return, migrants are accepted back into the traditional order. For some ethnic groups, migration has found its way into community traditions. Among the Tonga, whose male population is well over 50 percent migratory, a young boy's first migration is considered a sign of manhood.

Independent Picture Service

Workers *(above)* pick tea leaves on a large plantation. In the mines of South Africa, a Malawian miner *(below)* drills for coal.

Courtesy of SATOUR

39

A Malawian woman and her children use wattle and daub (interwoven wood and clay) to construct a storage bin.

Western-style homes dot Blantyre.

Blantyre's modern Mount Soche Hotel overlooks traditional Malawian dwellings.

Housing

The most common building materials in rural areas are wattle and daub (frameworks of rods and twigs packed with clay), specially grown bamboo, and thatch. Frequently, homes are round and windowless, with thatched roofs and floors of packed earth. Most houses measure about eight feet in diameter.

Different ethnic groups have modified this basic design to suit their needs. The Yao first construct an outline of strong poles planted into the earth. This inner frame is then covered with another framework of hollow bamboo. The Ngoni design houses that taper upward at both ends—a shape that resembles a ship. Western and Arab influences, however, have changed building patterns in some areas. The Sena, for example, frequently put up rectangular houses with windows and paneled doors.

Rural buildings require constant upkeep. Within 5 to 10 years white ants will eat away the bamboo supports, and rain will crumble away the plaster. Furnishings for low-income rural dwellers are simple pieces made by local craftspeople. Wealthier rural inhabitants purchase deck chairs and rattan (cane) furniture.

The quality of urban housing depends on a person's income and ranges from shanties to modern, Western-style accommodations. Most laborers who come to cities in search of work leave their families behind in rural villages because urban living is costly. Even for shantytown dwellers, water can cost several cents per day, and a shanty with a corrugated tin roof may rent for half of the average laborer's monthly salary.

Government officials have developed a plan to accommodate the rush to the cities, whereby the state pays to supply an area with roads, water, and outhouses. In return, renters build their own homes. Nevertheless, the spread of unhealthy shantytowns—and of the diseases that flourish in them—continues.

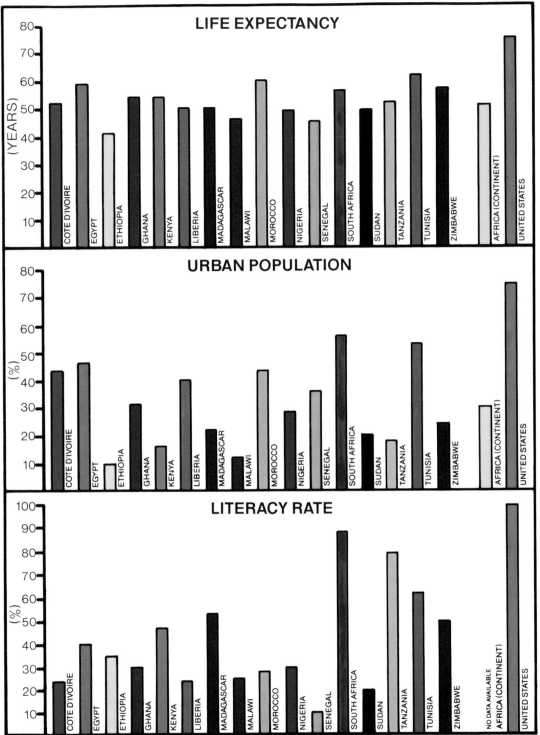

The three factors depicted in this graph suggest differences in the quality of life among 16 African nations. Averages for the United States and the entire continent of Africa are included for comparison. (Data taken from "1987 World Population Data Sheet" and *PC-Globe*.)

Health

Malawi's medical programs focus on curing, rather than preventing, disease. The Banda administration has made health a relatively low priority. The government spent less than 1 percent of its development budget on health improvements during the decade following independence. Since most of the country's doctors live and work in the cities, many rural people rely on traditional healers and herbalists.

A major portion of the country remains unsanitary and threatened by disease. The thatched roofs of houses support rats and insects, and livestock is often kept too close to wells, resulting in impure water. Most rural wells are checked once or twice a year by a mobile government mini-laboratory, but this has proved inadequate. Only urban residents are as yet assured of safe drinking water. Although malaria, the

second highest cause of death, is still a major threat, Blantyre is officially free of the mosquitoes that carry the disease.

Malawi's infant mortality rate was 157 per 1,000 live births in 1989. Among African nations only Mali and Sierra Leone recorded higher figures. Between 30 and 50 percent of all children born in Malawi die by the age of five. Nevertheless, new medical facilities have helped to lower the death rate, especially among young children, and it is now common to find four or five children in a family surviving to adulthood. Average life expectancy, however, is only 46 years. As a result, 47 percent of the population are under 15 years of age, and only 3 percent are over 65.

A long-standing problem with venereal disease among migrant workers and urban dwellers has grown more serious in the

Photo by Howard W. Mielke

Since most of Malawi's physicians practice in urban areas, many rural dwellers have to rely on medicines and tonics purchased at local markets.

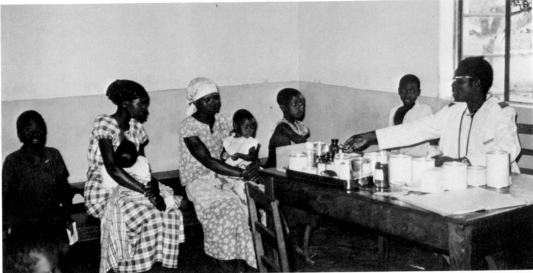

Photo by Paul and Bridget Martin

Rural clinics, although not a government priority, are growing in number and already have succeeded in curbing the nation's high infant mortality rate.

1980s with the spread of AIDS—acquired immune deficiency syndrome. Insufficient health information and substandard medical facilities have contributed to the spread of this epidemic disease. By 1989 more than 2,500 cases had been reported in Malawi, but the World Health Organization suspects that unreported cases may soon affect five million people throughout the continent.

Photo by Howard W. Mielke

Two men suffering from leprosy enjoy a game called *fuwa.* Leprosy still exists in Malawi, although instances of it grow rarer each year.

Courtesy of Library of Congress

Traditional healers—who combine herbal medicines with folklore—still live in remote parts of Malawi.

43

Fuwa is popular among children and adults and requires quick mental agility to win the opponent's playing pieces.

Photo by Howard W. Mielke

Education

More than 70 percent of Malawian boys and 49 percent of Malawian girls are enrolled in primary school, which is free and lasts eight years. Secondary schools have enlarged their curricula to include more technical and vocational subjects for those who seek skilled employment. Roughly 35 percent of the population are literate in Chichewa; considerably less are literate in English. Less than 10 percent of Malawians attend secondary school.

In addition to schools operated by missions, the British Voluntary Service Overseas and the U.S. Peace Corps supply

Men in Malawi have always had greater access to education than women. Even male migrant laborers, who leave their families in rural villages to work in cities, have had better opportunities to learn how to speak English and how to write Chichewa. In the mid-1980s the number of men literate in Chichewa was nearly double the number of literate women.

Courtesy of Malawi Department of Information

many teachers for the fast-growing secondary schools. Higher education is provided at the University of Malawi, which has five specialized colleges; at Kamuzu Academy, which opened in 1981; and at the Malawi Correspondence College. Five technical schools are also in operation.

In 1965 President Banda began the Malawi Young Pioneers movement. Since the country's economy is based on agriculture, the work of the Young Pioneers is concentrated in the rural areas. The training takes 10 months and covers a wide variety of subjects—agriculture, resettlement schemes, first aid, basic education, sports, and youth leadership techniques. After completing the training, Young Pioneers return to their villages where they pass on their knowledge to others. Mozambique asserts that the Young Pioneers are also trained in military tactics and that the group is used to aid Mozambican guerrilla fighters. The Malawian government denies such claims.

Photo by Howard W. Mielke

Organized athletics have a firm place in Malawian education. Soccer, called football, is the favorite national sport, although boxing, baseball, and basketball are also popular.

Courtesy of Malawi Department of Information

The creation of the Malawi Young Pioneers was one of President Banda's solutions to the poverty and isolation of rural populations. Young Pioneers are required to spend time in remote settlements and to pass on the knowledge that they gain from their training.

Ivory was historically an important commodity for Malawian traders. Craftspeople learned to carve the valuable material into intricate designs. Small statues *(left)*, along with thin letter openers *(below)*, are traditional objects. Ivory hunters continue to kill endangered elephants and rhinos to obtain their ivory tusks.

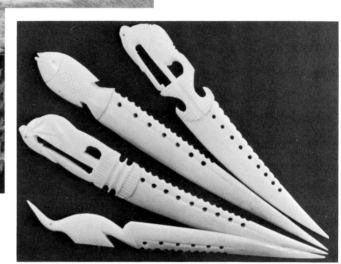

The Arts

Government control of the media in Malawi has severely restricted the production of major works of contemporary literature. Nevertheless, Aubrey Kachingwe's first novel, *No Easy Task*, explores the political struggles of a British colony moving toward independence. Legson Kayira's *The Detainee* is a tragic novel about an old man harassed by a youth brigade in an imaginary African country. In recent years, the works of several Malawian poets—including David Rubadiri—have drawn worldwide attention.

Like most African nations, Malawi has a rich dance tradition, which combines many individual ethnic ceremonies. Most dances are accompanied by singing, playing, and rhythmic clapping. Although originally limited to certain ethnic groups, some dances have become known nationwide. *Gule wa mkulu* (the big dance), for example, was once connected to the crowning ceremonies of Chewa leaders. Parts of the dance also evolved from initiation funeral dances. Performers wear masks and feathered headgear and cover themselves with mud, ash, or animal skins.

Malawian musical instruments are usually carefully crafted by the performer. Most important are drums, which are sometimes combined to form large drum orchestras. Flutes, stringed instruments, and the *lipenga*, or singing horn—a wind instrument made from a specially treated gourd—are commonly used to accompany dancing.

Religion and Holidays

Roughly 50 percent of Malawians follow traditional African religious beliefs, 35 percent are Christian, and 15 percent are Muslim (followers of the Islamic religion). But religious influences have blended over

46

the years. Malawians who are Christians often continue to hold ethnic beliefs. Some African churches incorporate both Muslim and Christian symbols.

Traditional African religions revolve around the idea that all things—alive or dead, human or animal—are part of a vital life force. Deceased relatives and rulers are thought to watch over family and village affairs.

Although many Malawians still follow traditional ethnic beliefs, approximately one Malawian in three is Christian. Half of these are Roman Catholics. The Presbyterian Church of Central Africa is the largest Protestant group. These Christian churches have established institutions throughout the country and contribute greatly in the fields of education and medical service.

Hand-painted murals, showing the mutual influences of Christianity and local art forms, decorate a church at Chitala.

Photo by Howard W. Mielke

Stringed playing pieces, along with drums and horns, are quite often made by hand. This one-stringed instrument can be tuned to produce a number of musical notes.

Photo by Paul and Bridget Martin

Blantyre Mission Church, located outside the city of Blantyre, dates from the late nineteenth century. A remnant of European influence, the church displays an intricacy of construction that contrasts with simple African dwellings in the same area.

Photo by Howard W. Mielke

Open-air festivals often involve large groups of dancers. Births, deaths, harvests, and national holidays are all celebrated through dance.

Local markets provide an opportunity for subsistence farmers – those who grow food mainly for their families – to sell small amounts of extra produce or grain.

Flour, made from either maize (corn) or cassava (a root crop), is one of the subsistence farmer's most important staples. After the harvest, a two-step process is required to produce flour. First, the raw maize or cassava is pounded and crushed in a hollow drum, using long wooden poles *(above)*. Second, the crushed crop is carefully sifted to remove husks and other unwanted material *(right)*.

Malawians celebrate traditional Christian holidays, such as Christmas and Easter, as well as a few nonreligious days that are uniquely British, including Boxing Day (December 26). In addition, Malawi has three special holidays of its own—Martyr's Day, President Banda's birthday (called Kamuzu Day), and Republic Day. Faithful Muslims observe the daytime fast during the Islamic holy month of Ramadan.

Food

Although fish provides the population's chief source of animal protein, many families cannot afford to eat it very often. Like most Africans, Malawians eat local products, such as fruits, nuts, and grains. A typical Malawian meal consists of *nkhuani relishe* (pumpkin leaves cooked with tomatoes and peanuts), *nyama pamodzi ndi mbatata* (meat stewed with tomatoes, on-

Photo by Paul and Bridget Martin

Fish from Lake Malawi, arranged on sticks and smoked, are available at many local markets.

Courtesy of Save the Children

Most cooking in Malawi is done over an open fire. As a result, dishes that do not require controlled heating—such as fried or steamed foods—are popular.

50

Community storage bins *(left),* often serving an entire village, are elevated to keep the grain free of insects and small animals. Since the bins are usually placed in the center of the village, they provide a natural spot for group work or relaxation. Shelling peas by hand *(below)* is a typical group task.

ions, and potatoes), *nsima* (cornmeal porridge), and *guava okazinga* (fried guavas).

Malawians are very fond of sugarcane, and it is common to see children walking along the road sucking on a piece of cane as if it were a stick of candy. Beer is the national drink, but it is completely different from the brew known to people in Europe and North America. Malawian beer is so thick that it is more like a food than a beverage.

Rice threshing, the process of separating rice from the stalk, is a long, painstaking process.

51

Courtesy of F. Botts/FAO

Many farmers in Malawi use simple, traditional tools to work their small plots of land.

4) The Economy

In precolonial days, ivory and slaves were the main exports from Central Africa. When Europeans came to the area, they began to plant commercial crops, such as tobacco, tea, peanuts, and cotton. Today those agricultural products are Malawi's chief exports.

About 31 percent of Malawi's land is suitable for raising crops. Almost 24 percent of the land is covered with forests, and more than 6 percent is devoted to meadow and pasture. Over 36 percent of the nation's territory is made up of rugged mountains and rocky terrain without economic value. Much of the country suffers from water shortages throughout the year.

Financial aid from the United States and Great Britain has been used to develop a few private industries. Nevertheless, like most other nations, Malawi has suffered from a slowing of the world's economy in the 1980s. In addition, the rising prices of oil and industrial goods, combined with the declining prices paid for raw materials and export crops, have negatively affected Malawi's financial standing.

Agriculture

Malawian farmers must learn agricultural techniques that will help them to cope with weather changes, such as flooding and drought. For this reason, the Department of Agriculture sponsors agricultural courses that are attended by thousands of farmers. In addition, the department produces special radio broadcasts and distributes information leaflets to educate farmers.

Malawi continues to rank as a major exporter of fire-cured and sun-cured tobaccos. Some 50 million pounds of the crop are exported yearly, much of it to Great Britain. Many small-scale farmers grow tobacco, particularly near Kasungu, in the Central Region. The government runs laboratories that determine the quality of the tobacco, experiment in curing it, and test seeds.

Tea is the second largest export crop, and much of it is grown in the Mlanje district. Started in 1878, the tea industry today employs thousands of Malawians to pick the nearly 50,000 pounds of tea that are grown each year on large plantations. Because the plants thrive at high altitudes, they are an excellent crop for Malawi's plateaus and hillsides. More than 40,000 acres of Malawi's land are planted in tea, and estimates indicate that another 10,000 acres are suitable for growing tea.

Peanuts are important both as an export crop and as a local food source. Because they must be shelled and sorted by hand, peanuts require a great deal of manual labor. Plant diseases have also been a problem. Nevertheless, peanuts are a good crop to rotate with maize (corn) and tobacco, because they add nutrients to the soil.

About 90,000 acres of Malawi's fertile land produce cotton. Most cotton is cultivated in the Southern Region, but it is also being introduced as a rotation crop in the Central Region. The country produces more than 40,000 tons of sugar a year, which is enough to meet its own needs. More acres are now devoted to sugarcane

Courtesy of Malawi Department of Information

Tobacco *(above)* and tea *(below)* are well suited to the nation's climate. Both plants thrive in Malawi's fertile soil and bring steady prices on the world market. Also, both can be produced by small-scale landholders as well as on large plantations.

Courtesy of Malawi Department of Information

to answer the increasing demand in the country and to create a surplus for export.

Rice is grown in Malawi as a local food source, and, when a surplus exists, it is exported to nearby countries. Two million acres are devoted to beans, a rotation crop rich in protein. Cassavas (a fleshy root crop) have long been grown for local consumption but have now also become an important export item.

Forestry

Roughly 24 percent of the land area of Malawi is forested, although this figure includes a large amount of savanna woodland, which is only lightly forested. Woods are an important natural asset because they produce timber and protect the soil. Many small forests, mostly evergreen, thrive in the highlands and in the mountains. Some areas of the country support eucalyptus trees and special high-yield pines.

To meet the growing demand for timber and to lessen the need for importing it, the

Independent Picture Service

Small-scale farmers in the Central Region use cotton as a rotation crop—a plant that restores nutrients to the soil. Another way farmers revive overused land is by allowing a field to lie fallow, or unplanted, for several years.

government has started an active forestry scheme. Under this plan, 3,000 acres are planted with trees each year, mostly on the plateaus and high mountain slopes.

Photo by Paul and Bridget Martin

Sugarcane grows extremely tall as it ripens. When this crop is ready for harvest, laborers will cut it by hand, and the cane will then be processed at the factory across the field.

Palm trees grow primarily in the humid Southern Region of Malawi.

While logging is not a major industry in Malawi, a substantial amount of lumber is cut in the Mlanje Mountains each year.

The government owns most of the timber plantations, although private industry has increased its involvement in the forestry business. The Imperial Tobacco Group grows eucalyptus trees to supply timber for its tobacco boxes and has started to make plywood. The Forestry Department has planted about 34,000 acres of softwood trees. Separate plantations have been established on the northern Vipya Plateau to provide raw material for the pulp and paper industries. A pulp mill built near the railway at Salima (a central, lakeside district) enables Malawi to export wood pulp for packaging materials.

Fishing

Fish is the most important source of protein in the average Malawian's diet. The main fishing areas are Lake Chilwa, Lake Malombe, the southern end of Lake Malawi, and the lower reaches of the Shire River. Lake Malawi itself contains more than 200 species of fish, many of them found nowhere else in the world.

55

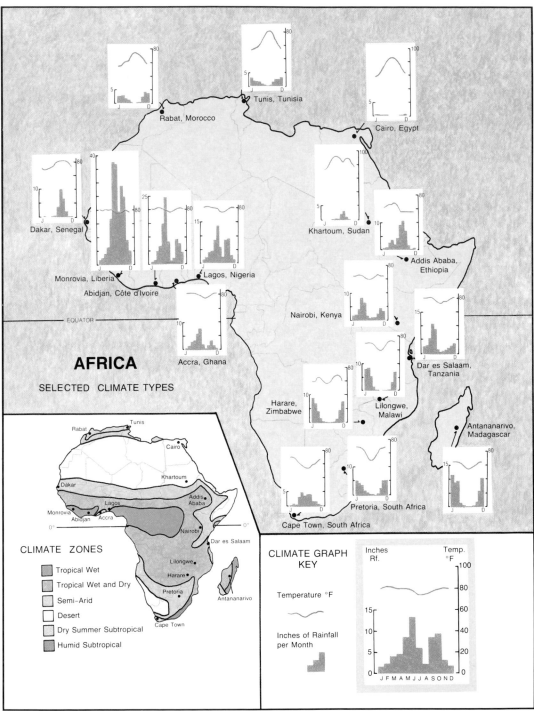

AFRICA

SELECTED CLIMATE TYPES

Rabat, Morocco

Tunis, Tunisia

Cairo, Egypt

Dakar, Senegal

Khartoum, Sudan

Addis Ababa, Ethiopia

Monrovia, Liberia

Abidjan, Côte d'Ivoire

Lagos, Nigeria

Accra, Ghana

Nairobi, Kenya

Dar es Salaam, Tanzania

EQUATOR

Harare, Zimbabwe

Lilongwe, Malawi

Antananarivo, Madagascar

Pretoria, South Africa

Cape Town, South Africa

CLIMATE ZONES

- Tropical Wet
- Tropical Wet and Dry
- Semi–Arid
- Desert
- Dry Summer Subtropical
- Humid Subtropical

Rabat
Tunis
Cairo
Khartoum
Dakar
Addis Ababa
Lagos
Monrovia
Abidjan
Accra
Nairobi
Dar es Salaam
Lilongwe
Harare
Pretoria
Antananarivo
Cape Town

CLIMATE GRAPH KEY

Inches Rf.

Temp. °F

Temperature °F

Inches of Rainfall per Month

J F M A M J J A S O N D

Artwork by Carol F. Barrett

These climate graphs show the monthly change in the average rainfall received and in the average temperature from January to December for the capital cities of 16 African nations. Lilongwe, Malawi, has a fairly typical tropical wet and dry climate. A strong contrast exists between the cool, dry winter (May through September) and the hot, wet summer months. (Data taken from *World-Climates* by Willy Rudloff, Stuttgart, 1981.)

Fishing techniques have changed greatly in the late twentieth century. Plank boats with outboard motors are now used instead of dugout canoes with paddles. Fishing companies have adopted large-scale trawling methods. As a result, total catches have nearly doubled in the last 15 years, rising from 40,000 tons in the late 1960s to over 70,000 tons by the 1980s.

A fish cannery has been built at Salima, and a cold-storage plant has been established at Fort Johnston. The most popular fish for canning are chambo and *nchila*, which resemble perch and carp, respectively. At least 10,000 Malawians make their living in the fishing industry. Fishermen take their catch to market by bicycle, truck, or bus.

Mining and Manufacturing

Important bauxite deposits (the principal source of aluminum) exist near Mlanje. Despite several plans for transporting the mined bauxite ore—including one for liquefying it and shipping it to plants via pipeline—the Malawian government has not significantly expanded the industry. Uranium—a raw material for producing nuclear energy—exists in undetermined amounts. Diamonds and rare metallic elements, such as lanthanum, are mined, and a Malawian firm has started a small industry based on the production of gem-quality corundum (the raw material used to produce rubies and sapphires). Limestone provides the key ingredient for a thriving national cement industry.

The aim of the manufacturing industry is to produce articles from the raw materials that are grown in Malawi. Immediately after independence, industrial development in Malawi was extremely rapid, with a growth rate of 17 percent per year. The increase of farm products—tea, tobacco, peanuts, rice, and sugar—that require processing has helped to speed up the growth of such processing industries.

Courtesy of Malawi High Commission

Fishermen often use a single, hand-thrown net to make their day's catch. Rocks are fastened to parts of the net to help it sink to a depth where the fish feed.

Much of Malawi's new industrial technology, like these automated weaving machines, requires skilled labor. Consequently, schools are placing more and more emphasis on vocational instruction.

The making of pulp and paper has become an important industry, but in most other sectors of the economy, growth has slowed in recent years.

Much of Malawi's early development as a nation can be traced to its ties with South Africa. In 1973 South Africa supplied 13 percent of Malawi's imports and bought 5 percent of all its exports. By the late 1980s imports had increased significantly, with Malawi buying 38 percent of its foreign goods from South Africa.

Transportation

Malawi has four main transportation systems—road, rail, air, and water. Only a small percentage of the 7,028 miles of roads are paved, but they are constantly extended and improved. The road network

A brick factory in Limbe produces rough but solid building blocks.

Air Malawi runs regularly scheduled jet flights to several nations in East Africa.

Train travel and transport have suffered in recent years as a result of guerrilla attacks on the rail lines that Malawi shares with war-torn Mozambique.

already links Malawi with Mozambique, Zimbabwe, Zambia, and Tanzania. In addition, Malawi has railway access to Mozambique's Indian Ocean ports, its chief means of shipping exports to foreign markets.

Government-owned Air Malawi has regularly scheduled flights, both within the country and to African nations such as Zimbabwe, Mozambique, Zambia, Kenya, and South Africa. Many other airlines have regular flights to and from the international airports near Blantyre and Li-

longwe. A fleet of ships carrying both cargo and passengers operates on Lake Malawi. The fleet's headquarters at Monkey Bay features a dockyard and other facilities.

Transportation for the average rural dweller continues to mean walking. Cars and trucks are too expensive to own and to fuel with imported gasoline. Bicycles, though increasingly more common, are still considered luxuries. For those who live in the south—particularly along the shores of Lake Malawi—bus systems are

Several companies provide transportation on Lake Malawi. Boats crossing the lake are as crowded—and nearly as frequent—as buses are in the city.

relatively dependable and inexpensive. In general, inhabitants of the north travel without the convenience of modern transportation.

The Nkula Falls hydropower facility supplies electricity to Blantyre.

Energy

Hydroelectric power has steadily replaced coal from Zimbabwe and oil from the Middle East as Malawi's chief source of energy for industry. While road transport still depends on imported fuel, over 70 percent of Malawi's electricity now comes from water-driven turbines. Gas-driven turbines supply the remaining 30 percent. Electricity consumption has grown at the rate of 20 percent a year and is controlled through a single public agency, the Electrical Supply Commission of Malawi.

Future energy sources may include development of northern coal deposits, which were too remote from roads to be worth extracting in the 1980s. Several more hydroelectric plants are planned for the Shire River. The production of ethanol (alcohol fuel made from sugar) has increased every year since manufacturing began in 1982. Ethanol now replaces 20 percent of Malawi's petroleum imports.

Tourism

Malawi has fine national parks with diverse wildlife. These parks attract hundreds of visitors and add greatly to the economy of the country. In the far southwest is 50-acre Lengwe National Park, the smallest of the nation's game reserves. Large numbers of nyalas—a rare species of antelope—roam freely in the region but are not found farther north in Africa. A 40-mile circular drive, with many branch roads, enables visitors to see animals in their natural grazing areas and at their regular watering holes.

Located on the western borders of the Central Region, Kasungu National Park covers 800 square miles of rolling savanna. It is the largest of Malawi's parks and contains a wide range of animal life. A third game park, Nyika National Park, covers 360 square miles and is found in northwestern Malawi. About 90 percent of the park is savanna, with evergreen forests covering the rest. Scattered peaks rising

Photo by Howard W. Mielke

The royal poinciana is more commonly called the flamboyant tree, in recognition of its vivid colors.

over 5,000 feet add contrast to the landscape. Throughout the year, large herds of eland, zebras, roan antelope, duikers, and reedbuck roam the grasslands.

Courtesy of Malawi High Commission

The nyala—a shy and rare species of antelope—is found only in Malawi.

Craftspeople, like this carpenter, and small manufacturers are a major force in Malawi's limited industrial base.

Outlook for the Future

Malawi is often portrayed as one of the few African countries that, since independence, has combined economic progress with political stability. Unlike most other nations on the continent, Malawi has retained agriculture as the backbone of its economy rather than developing an industrial base. This strategy has made Malawi self-sufficient in food production but has slowed its growth in other economic areas.

Banda and his associates have prospered under the strict, one-party system that has existed since independence. Critics of the president maintain that his policies, which encourage rural farmers to sell their crops instead of consuming them, have worsened the living standards of village populations. On the national level, the Banda administration's support of white-minority governments has isolated Malawi from its neighbors. Mozambique, whose railways hold the key to Malawi's economic success, is only one of many African nations whose relations with Malawi are strained.

Banda shows signs of changing his controversial foreign policies, however. In 1986, for example, he authorized the establishment of a joint security commission with Mozambique, and he openly criticized South Africa in the Western press. By continuing to improve relations with its neighbors, Malawi may be able to overcome its economic handicap of being landlocked. Much will depend on Banda's successor, who will need to cultivate both the popular support that Banda has had and the partnership with neighboring countries that Banda has let slip away.

Photo by Paul and Bridget Martin

President Banda moves through a gathering of Malawian women toward a speaker's platform. Because political resistance is illegal within Malawi's borders, opposition to Banda is limited to a small number of political organizations stationed in neighboring countries.

Index